# Th~ Lobster's Birthday

## and Other Stories

Compiled by Catherine Baker

## Contents

OXFORD
UNIVERSITY PRESS

# Harriet's Story

## by Morris Gleitzman

Harriet wakes up.

She can't see anything except the dull glow of her bedside clock.

3.14 am.

That explains why the rest of her bedroom is dark. Darker than the inside of a black sock that's been swallowed by a large bat who lives in a cave with very thick curtains.

Strange, thinks Harriet. I don't usually wake up in the middle of the night. And if I do, I don't usually lie here making up weird sentences about how dark it is.

She wonders what's going on.

Then she realizes.

She's thirsty. Very thirsty. Thirstier than a blast-furnace operator lost in the middle of the Sahara desert who forgot to have a drink before he went on holiday.

Of course, thinks Harriet. That's why I've woken up. And that's why I'm making up these weird sentences. My brain's dehydrated.

Easily fixed.

Harriet switches on her lamp and reaches for the glass of water Mum always leaves on the bedside table.

The glass is empty. Emptier than a cave whose usual inhabitant, a large hungry sock-eating bat, has rushed off to the Sahara after hearing that an overheated blast-furnace operator has just taken off his shoes.

Harriet blinks.

This thirst, she thinks, is really making me think weird things.

Oh well, still easily fixed.

Plenty to drink in the kitchen. Water in the tap. Juice in the fridge. Long-life milk in the cupboard if I feel like a long life.

Harriet gets out of bed, opens her bedroom door and creeps out. She closes the door quietly behind her.

The hallway isn't as dark as her room. There's a faint haze of moonlight coming through a window.

This is more sort of gloomy than dark, thinks Harriet. As gloomy as a bat in the desert staring at two socks it can't eat because it's allergic to polyester.

Stop it, Harriet says to herself.

The kitchen.

She doesn't turn the hallway light on. Mustn't wake Mum and Dad. They both work hard and need their sleep.

As Harriet creeps past their room, she hears gentle snoring. And wheezing. And slobbering.

Muttley must be sleeping on their bed.

Just the thought of her beloved dog makes Harriet's insides go warm. Almost as warm as the polyester-sock soup a hungry bat might make to try and get some of the sock flavour without having to swallow any of the actual ...

Harriet concentrates on getting down the stairs to the kitchen.

Luckily there are some glints of moonlight on the stairs. She goes down carefully, step by step, counting each stair silently to keep her mind from wandering.

... three, four, five ...

She stops.

Gleaming on the next stair is a small plastic racing car.

Typical, she thinks. Younger brothers always leave their toys where other people could step on them and do triple backward somersaults down the stairs and land on their pelvises and sprain their anterior fibulate cartilages and miss out on selection for the school swimming team.

Harriet reminds herself that Billy is only four and probably didn't mean it.

Then the moonlight disappears.

The plastic racing car glows eerily. Particularly around the headlights.

Strange.

Harriet didn't think racing cars had headlights.

She stands in the darkness, feeling a bit spooked. She's read about this. Hallucinations. Seeing things. It can happen to people who are extremely thirsty. She read a story only recently about somebody dying of thirst in a desert who thought a large bat was eating his socks.

Mum. Dad. Help.

Harriet wants to call out. She wants Mum and Dad to wake up and switch on the light and stumble concerned out of their room and trip over Muttley and do triple backward somersaults down the stairs and land on their pelvises and sprain their anterior fibulate cartilages and miss out on ...

No, she doesn't.

It's OK, Harriet tells herself. I'm not in the desert. I'm standing on the stairs at home. People don't usually die of thirst standing on the stairs, even when they feel like they might.

Slowly, carefully, she moves down the dark steps towards the kitchen.

... eleven, twelve, thirteen ...

She knows there are fifteen steps because that's how Mum and Dad taught her to count, years ago. But she prepares herself for a few more now, maybe a few hundred more, because that's what happens when you're hallucinating from thirst.

… fourteen, fifteen …

She tests ahead with her foot.

No more.

Just flat floor.

Good, the hallucinations have stopped.

Harriet walks towards the kitchen, very slowly and carefully because this downstairs hall is darker than a …

Stop that.

She can't see the kitchen door, but she knows roughly how far it is from the bottom of the stairs. She holds her hands up in front of her in case the hallucinations start again and she bumps into a stuffed gorilla or a big pile of bat poo or the Eiffel Tower.

Bump.

Her fingers are touching something. It doesn't feel lumpy or pooey or French.

It feels like a door handle.

Yes.

The kitchen door.

At last she can get a drink.

Harriet turns the handle, steps into the kitchen and quietly closes the door. Now she can switch the light on without disturbing Mum and Dad.

She does.

At first, the brightness hurts her eyes. She can't see anything. All she can think of is thirst. She wants to rush to the fridge and grab the bottle of juice and glug it down, blind and squinting. But she doesn't.

There are other bottles and jars in the fridge she wouldn't want to grab by mistake. Soy sauce. Dad's home-made ginger beer.

Instead Harriet turns away from the glare and waits for her eyes to adjust. Which they do. Soon she can see the back of the kitchen door clearly.

She can also see a big shadow looming over her.

Somebody else is in the kitchen.

Somebody big.

From the shape of the shadow, it doesn't look like Mum or Dad or Billy. It looks like a man with the sort of very broad shoulders a burglar would probably have. And over one of his shadow shoulders is what looks like a huge sack. Bulging with something very big inside it.

Probably the fridge, thinks Harriet.

She wants to run.

She wants to claw open the kitchen door and leap up the stairs and fling herself into bed with Mum and Dad.

But her hands are sweaty with fear and she knows that if she tries to grab the door handle her fingers will probably slip and she'll be fumbling and the burglar will have heaps of time to grab her and put her in his sack.

She has to think of something else.

Behind her, the burglar isn't saying anything.

He's probably in shock too, thinks Harriet. Burglars are probably cowards underneath, which is why they slink around stealing fridges in the dark.

Harriet has an idea. She decides to turn and face the burglar and pretend she's braver than she is. She'll offer him a deal. If she can have the juice, he can take the fridge.

She turns, guts twisted tighter than a polyester sock. And blinks.

There isn't a burglar.

Just Mum's ski suit, hanging from the light fitting. The hood has flopped over to one side and is making a big sack-shaped shadow.

Harriet remembers Mum saying the ski suit has to go to the drycleaners. She must have hung it here so she wouldn't forget.

Dizzy with relief and thirst, Harriet pulls the fridge door open, almost tasting the cool sweet juice.

She grabs the juice bottle.

It's empty.

So's the milk.

Dad's ginger beer fermentation jar is lying broken in

the bottom of the fridge. Most of the ginger beer has leaked out and been soaked up by the leftover curry and rice in the salad crisper.

Harriet stares, horrified.

There's only one person who'd drink everything in the fridge that carelessly.

Harriet knows she should be waking Mum and Dad and telling them the bad news so they can inform the insurance company and get some more ginger beer yeast for Dad and call the police to see if there's a Younger Brother Punishment Squad.

But first she absolutely must have a drink.

Harriet grabs a glass from the cupboard and goes to the sink and turns the tap on.

Nothing comes out.

She turns the tap on more. Still nothing. She tries the hot tap. Nothing.

The taps are completely dry. Drier than a pair of socks that have been lying in the desert sun so long you wouldn't even know a bat had tried to make soup out of them.

Oh no, thinks Harriet. I'm making up weird sentences again.

Another thought hits her.

Is it just a coincidence the fridge is empty and the water pipes are dry on the same night? Or is something else going on?

Like ...

Like ...

Harriet can't imagine what it could be. She thinks about the moonlight disappearing, and the plastic racing car going spooky, and the burglar-shaped shadow. And now suddenly here's a drought or a burst water main or a clogged valve at the reservoir. Everything that's happened since she got out of bed has made it harder for her to get a drink.

Getting a drink should be so simple.

Not a big problem.

Unless ...

Suddenly Harriet has to sit down on a kitchen chair.

Could it be ...?

Last week in class Ms Lovett was talking about stories and how they work. How in every story, the main character must have a problem. And how the character never solves the problem straight away, because that would make the story too short and too boring.

'In a story,' Ms Lovett said, 'things always come along to make the problem harder to solve. Things always get worse before they get better.'

Harriet thinks again about the empty glass and the racing car and the dark hall and scary shadow and the empty juice bottle and the dry taps.

Could it be, she thinks, that I'm in a story?

No, that's crazy.

Harriet goes to the cupboard, finds the long-life milk and opens the carton. She tips the milk into the glass. Except she doesn't because nothing comes out. She shakes the carton. The contents feel solid. And now there's a cheesy smell.

She looks more closely at the carton to make sure Mum didn't buy long-life cheese by mistake. No, it says long-life milk. Right next to where it says *Use By September 2009*.

Harriet puts the carton down.

She's tempted to ring Ms Lovett for advice. But it's 3.25 am and she knows teachers don't get paid overtime.

No, thinks Harriet, I'll deal with this myself.

She remembers something else Ms Lovett said.

As characters battle to solve their problems, they often discover they're braver than they ever thought they were.

Harriet isn't feeling particularly brave at the moment but definitely more determined.

And thirstier.

My problem, she says to herself, is getting a drink. If I'm in a story, things will keep coming along to make it harder for me to solve my problem.

Let's put it to the test.

Harriet thinks about what she can do next.

Of course. If a person finds themself in a drinkless kitchen, there's an obvious solution. Go out into the garden and drink from the fish pond.

Harriet opens the kitchen window and peers out. The moon is glowing again and the pond is rippling, but the trees around it are full of bats.

They're fruit bats and Harriet knows they're harmless, but she also knows it's best not to drink anything that's directly under a bat's bottom.

She closes the window.

OK, she thinks. I need another way to fix the problem. How about waking up Mum and Dad and asking them to drive me to the all-night supermarket? It's only a ten-minute journey.

Harriet takes a couple of steps towards the stairs, then stops.

She's thinking of all the things that could happen on the way to the supermarket to stop her solving her problem.

Dad crashing the car into the library.

The whole family being abducted by aliens and taken to a planet where the inhabitants live on a diet of really salty crisps and curried sand.

Mum being pulled over for not wearing a seatbelt and then being charged with the desert murder of a sockless blast-furnace operator.

Mind you, there would probably be a water cooler at the police station ...

No.

Harriet sits down again and thinks hard. She needs a way of solving her problem that won't put Mum and Dad in danger and cause them to lose sleep and / or their car and / or their freedom and / or their library tickets.

Of course, she says to herself. Why didn't I think of it before? I'll break into our neighbours' house and borrow a drink from them.

Harriet creeps out the back door, staying well away from the fruit bats, climbs over the fence and runs, crouching, across the neighbours' lawn.

At their house, trying to feel braver than she ever has before, she looks for a possible place to break in.

And finds one. An open toilet window. It's a bit high up, but if she stands on this garden table and pulls herself up using this metal box screwed to the wall with the little red flickering light on it ...

Oops, thinks Harriet as she jumps back down from the table. That burglar alarm wasn't there last time I looked.

Yet another thing making her problem harder to solve.

As Harriet hurries away from the neighbours' house,

she remembers something else Ms Lovett said about stories. How trying to solve a problem can sometimes cause an even bigger problem.

She also remembers something Dad said about the neighbours. How they collect Olympic swimming medals, buying them from all over the world and how they're always worrying that their priceless collection will be burgled.

That would have been a bigger problem all right, thinks Harriet. If the neighbours had caught me in their house and thought I was trying to steal their medals and had rung the police. The Older Sister Crime Squad would have been round in a flash.

As Harriet crosses the lawn, she notices that a trench has recently been dug and filled in again. A trench from the street to the neighbours' house.

A cable's probably been laid, she thinks. A high-security burglar alarm cable that has to go under the ground.

Wait a minute.

When a deep high-security trench is dug, perhaps it can sometimes damage other things under the ground. Like water pipes.

Harriet hurries out to the street, to where the trench meets the footpath. She peers at the ground. And sees exactly what she was hoping to see.

A big patch of damp mud.

She's so thirsty now she's tempted just to fill her mouth with mud and see if she can suck any water out of it.

But she doesn't. She hurries to the shed, finds Dad's pickaxe, comes back and digs down into the mud.

Yes.

There it is.

Just as she'd suspected.

She's uncovered the place where the water pipe to her house joins the main pipe for the street. In the house pipe, near the join, is a crack with water trickling out of it.

Harriet drops to her knees and laps at the water. It's muddy and gritty, but she doesn't care.

All she cares about is there's not enough of it.

The tantalizing taste of water is driving her crazy with thirst.

She grabs the pickaxe and swings it gently and makes the crack in the pipe just a little bit bigger. Mud and plastic putty ooze out of the crack.

Look at that, thinks Harriet. When they dug the trench, they not only cracked our pipe, they tried to hide what they'd done with plastic putty.

She swings the pickaxe again and makes the crack a little bit bigger again.

Well, quite a bit bigger actually, but Harriet doesn't care because now the water is bubbling out in a glorious fountain and she plunges her face into it and drinks and drinks and drinks.

And drinks.

Ahhhh, that's better.

Problem solved.

Suddenly Harriet is dizzy with tiredness. She has just enough strength to block the hole in the pipe with the putty and her socks, put the pickaxe back in the shed and drag herself up to bed.

She flops down and closes her eyes and as the warm tide of sleep carries her away, she has one last thought.

That's nice, she murmurs to herself. My story has a happy ending.

So deep is Harriet's sleep she doesn't hear the faint pop of a plug of putty and sock being expelled from a hole in a water pipe and the soft gush of water fountaining high into the night sky and then cascading down a driveway and under the neighbours' front door.

Hours later she's still slumbering so soundly that even the harsh sound of a State Emergency Service diesel pump starting up on the other side of the fence doesn't wake her. Nor does the even harsher sound of the neighbours wailing about possible rust damage to their medals.

Somebody the noise does wake, though, in the next street, is Ms Lovett.

Hmmm, thinks Ms Lovett, stretching sleepily under the covers with the contentment of a person who loves her job. I think I'll talk to the class some more about stories today. Introduce them to irony.

Perhaps use the example of a character solving a problem and causing another problem that's the exact opposite.

She pauses, reflecting. Are they ready for irony, this lot? She stretches again, smiling. Yes, I think so.

# Cuts

## by Russell Hoban

Cuts! Don't talk to me about cuts. With London Transport and the NHS you expect it, but dreams for God's sake! I mean your own personal dreams that you dream in your own personal sleep in the privacy of your own home.

My name is Higgins, Clarence Higgins. You want chapter and verse, I'll give you chapter and verse. One night I was in this dream – not even a first showing, but a repeat. We'd got to the part where I was on the Wimbledon train and I saw someone reading an *Evening Standard* and the headline was HIGGINS MISSING. I moved closer for a better look and there was nothing else on the front page, nothing at all under the headline. The first time I had this dream there was a bit of story, continued on page two, about how I went missing and what led up to it – I remember that quite well.

'Excuse me, please,' I said to the man reading it. I took the paper and turned it round to see what he'd been reading and the spread facing him was perfectly blank! Not a word on it. 'Look at that,' I said to him. He was the same man who'd been reading the paper in this dream the first time round. 'That's just not good enough, is it?' I said. 'They're not paying proper attention to detail any more. Would you mind standing up and turning around for me?' He stood up and turned around and it was as I'd suspected – the back of him was just as blank as the inside of the *Evening Standard*.

'This is too much,' I said. 'It really is too much.'

'It's no use complaining to me,' he said. 'I just go where I'm sent and do as I'm told. I mean, I'm lucky to get the work, ain't I? There's lots of us has had nothing at all for weeks and weeks.'

'Lucky to get the work! You're only half a man – the back of you is a total blank and you're just going to accept that, are you?'

'What can I do about it?'

'Who's the Secretary of State for Dreams?'

'I haven't a clue. I always thought it was a local authority thing,' he said, and vanished as I woke up.

'Did you hear that?' I said to Gladys, she's my wife. 'They cut me off in the middle of a conversation, just like that.'

'It was only a dream, Clarence.'

'Only a dream! Everything's falling apart and you lie

there and say it's only a dream. Now that I think of it, there weren't even any sound effects in that tube train, nothing but that miserable bit of dialogue. And nothing visible outside the carriage windows. Nobody cares about doing things right anymore.'

Later that day I rang up the Borough of Hammersmith and Fulham. 'Who's in charge of dreams?' I said.

'I'll see if I can find out,' said the telephonist. I held while she made her enquiries. When she came back on to the line she said, 'There doesn't seem to be anyone. Are you awake or asleep?'

'Awake.'

'Try again later when you're asleep. They may be able to help you then.'

Easier said than done: every night in my dreams I rang them up and every time I got an engaged signal. And the phone boxes[1] I used! Some of them were only two-dimensional, with telephones like pieces of flat cardboard. The streets were filled with fronts and sides of cars and buses – if you didn't look at them from a certain angle the illusion of reality was gone. And the people! Profiles only, most of them. Full-face here and there. I knew better than to look at their backs as they passed. All right, I said to myself, we'll see about this.

---

[1] A public telephone.

When the going gets tough, the tough dream a visit to the Town Hall.

I thought it best to avoid public transport in this dream; I hailed a sort of fake-looking cab and when I was in it I saw that there was no driver and I had to keep pushing with one foot to make it go, like a child's scooter.

When I finally got to the Town Hall, I asked the receptionist for Dreams and she said, 'Third floor'. I didn't trust the lifts; I went two at a time up stairs that disappeared behind me until I found *Dream Planning and Development*. There were several people at drawing tables and one pale profile of a man walking about in a supervisory sort of way. I tried to stay full-face but I could feel myself going flat and sideways.

'All right, you lot,' I said. 'What's going on here?'

'What's the problem?' said Mr Profile.

'You know jolly well what the problem is! Look around you at the way this dream is being conducted. You should be ashamed of yourselves.'

'What's your postcode?'

I told him.

'Name?'

I told him.

He went to a computer terminal and danced his fingers over the keyboard. I looked over his shoulder at the screen but all I could see was a row of Xs. 'Ah, well!' he said. 'I'm surprised you've been getting any dreams at all.'

'Why?' I could feel a coldness in the pit of my stomach.

'Well, you know they've halved our funding this year and we've had to cut back on everything. What I'm saying is, we've shut down the whole dream operation on your street and you've been made redundant.'

'Thanks very much,' I said. 'I'll see myself out.'

But I couldn't. No stairs, no lifts – just the merest sketch of a Town Hall interior and it went all dim and silent. Sometimes I'd catch a glimmer of someone but even when their mouths moved I couldn't hear anything and then they'd be gone. That was how long ago? Days? Months? Years? I'm not sure.

I don't know how much longer I can hold out here. I've tried to send this dream to Gladys but I'm not strong enough and in any case the dreams aren't running in our street any more. All I can hope for is that she'll move to some place where they are and then maybe she can dream me home.

But I don't know – it looks pretty bad from where I stand. Not that I'm standing, actually. If I wake up, or if you wake up – I'm not sure which – I expect these words will disappear.

# Aunt Arabelle in Charge

## by Richmal Crompton

The news that Ginger's parents were going abroad for a fortnight was received by Ginger and his friends, the Outlaws, with an exhilaration that they strove in vain to hide.

'We'll have the conservatory for our jungle camp,' said Ginger.

'And we'll play Alpine Sports on the front stairs,' said William.

'We can get up a bear hunt with the rug from the drawing room,' said Douglas.

'And we can have a *fine* time with those African weapons in your father's dressing-room,' said Henry.

Ginger, not wishing to seem too unfilial, added: 'I'm sorry they're goin', of course, but it isn't as if they weren't comin' back.'

'An', after all, it's only a fortnight,' said Henry. ''An' we'll put all the things back again so's they'll never know we've had them.'

Their exhilaration was slightly damped when they heard that an aunt of Ginger's, who had not seen Ginger since he was a baby, was coming to keep house in his parents' absence.

'If she's like *some* aunts ...' said William, speaking with gloom and bitterness from an exhaustive acquaintance of those relatives.

'She may be all right,' said Ginger. 'She writes things for papers.'

The spirits of the Outlaws rose again. They had met several people who wrote things for papers and had found them refreshingly absent-minded and conveniently blind to their immediate surroundings.

'She'll prob'ly never notice what we're doin',' said William. 'If she's like some of 'em she'll watch us doin' Alpine Sports down the front stairs an' never know we're there at all.'

'I hope so,' said Ginger, 'cause my mother's goin' to give me ten shillings when she comes back, if my aunt says I've been good.'

They showed signs of interest and excitement at this news. It was the custom of the Outlaws to have all things in common, especially tips.

'Oh, we'll get that ten shillin's all right,' said William confidently. 'She'll be so busy writin' soppy tales that she'll be as good as blind an' deaf.'

The appearance of Ginger's aunt was certainly reassuring.

She was a small, short-sighted woman with ink-stained fingers and untidy hair. She took her duties in, what Ginger considered, a very proper spirit.

'I'm a busy woman, dear boy,' she said to him, 'and I simply can't be disturbed at my work, so you must try not to bother me with *anything*. Just look after yourself and solve your own little problems as best you can. There's no reason why we should trouble each other at all except in case of an absolute *crisis*.'

So Ginger looked after himself and solved his own little problems and, on the whole, solved them very well. The problems consisted chiefly of how to turn the conservatory into a jungle, how to organize a really good bear hunt with the aid of the drawing room hearthrug and Ginger's father's treasured assegais[1] and how to make the staircase into a satisfactory Alpine Sports ground.

The last problem was solved by placing mattresses down the length of the staircase. William and Ginger became expert skiers, Henry was content to climb up and down with the aid of Ginger's father's alpenstock[2] and Douglas' speciality was rolling down it inside an empty linen basket.

---

[1] A type of spear.

[2] A type of walking stick.

William, who had written a play that had been acted by his followers and a serial story that had been published in a newspaper of his own editorship, and who therefore considered himself a full-fledged member of the profession of letters, took a great interest in Aunt Arabelle's activities.

'You tell her I'll help her if she gets stuck in a tale,' he said to Ginger, 'tell her I'm jolly good at writin' tales. Well, I've never read a better tale than that one I wrote called: "The Bloody Hand".'

'I have,' said Ginger.

'I bet you haven't,' said William. 'It's the best tale anyone's ever written. I wrote it, so I ought to *know*.'

It occurred to William that it would be a kind action if he added a few helpful touches to Aunt Arabelle's manuscript while she was out taking her daily 'constitutional', as a pleasant surprise for her on her return.

'I bet I can write about ghosts moanin' an' rattlin' chains as well as anyone,' he said.

'P'raps she doesn't write that sort of tale,' objected Ginger.

'Then I can write about dead bodies and findin' who killed 'em.'

'There's other sorts of tales than that,' said Ginger.

'No, there isn't,' said William firmly, 'not that

anyone ever wants to read, anyway.'

But an exhaustive search of Aunt Arabelle's desk revealed no stories of any sort – only a typewritten sheet headed: 'Answers to Correspondents'.

The first was: 'I am sorry, dear, that he has not spoken yet. But just go on being your own sweet self and I am sure he will soon.'

'What's that mean?' said Ginger with a mystified frown.

'It's someone who's got a dumb child an' is tryin' to cure it,' explained William in all good faith. 'What's the next?'

'I understand so well, Pansy dear,' read on Douglas, 'the anguish and turmoil that lives beneath the brave front you turn to the world. Probably he feels the same. Couldn't you find some mutual friend to introduce you? Then I am sure all will be well.'

'What's that mean?' said Ginger, looking still more mystified.

William himself looked puzzled for a minute. Finally enlightenment seemed to come.

'It's someone what's got stomach-ache an' she's tellin' 'em to get to know a doctor what's got stomach-ache too, so's he'll know how to cure her. It's a jolly good idea. I often wish our doctor had stomach-ache when I have it. I bet he'd try'n' find a nicer medicine if he'd gotter take it himself.'

The next day, William boldly tackled Aunt Arabelle on her literary work, kindly offering to give his help if she wished to turn her art to fiction.

'I've written some jolly good tales,' he said, 'an' I wouldn't mind helpin' you a bit.'

'No, thank you, dear boy,' said Aunt Arabelle. 'You see, I don't go in for fiction.'

'It's much more interestin' than writin' to people about dumbness an' stomach-ache,' said William.

'But I don't do that, dear. I help them in their little troubles of the heart.'

'Well, I think diseases are all dull,' said William, 'whether they're heart or stomach-ache or anything else. What do you write them for?'

'For a little paper called *Woman's Sphere*. I don't only do the Answers to Correspondents, of course. I sometimes do interviews. But,' she sighed, 'it's difficult to get *really* interesting people to be interviewed for the *Woman's Sphere*. It's only a twopenny, you see.'

But William, whose literary experience was confined to fiction, had lost interest in her work, though, liking always to be up to date, he made a mental note that Answers to Correspondents should form a part of the next paper he edited.

'I don't think much of her,' he said to Ginger, 'writing rot like that about hearts an' stomachs an' dumbness an' things.'

'She's better than any of your aunts, anyway,' said Ginger, feeling that the honour of his family must be defended.

'Oh, is she?' said William, accepting the challenge. 'All right, you tell me one of my aunts she's better than.'

'The one that asked why they only used one goal post at a time when she came to see the rugger match.'

'Oh, is she? Well, let me tell you she's not. I'd sooner have her than one that writes rot about hearts an' stomachs an' dumbness.'

'*An*' the one that told your father that it was wrong to take life in any form and that greenfly had as much right to existence as he had.'

The argument degenerated from this point into a discussion on aunts in general and finally took the form of a rivalry for queerness in aunts, from which Ginger emerged triumphant with Aunt Arabelle.

The pursuits, however, that had been so exciting during the first few days of her visit soon began to pall. The conservatory had its limitations as a jungle, the hunt with assegais proved interesting only to a certain point (assegais were unwieldy weapons and prone to bite the hand that fed them) and, though Alpine Sports on the staircase retained their charm the longest, their delights too were exhausted before the end of the first week.

Then the Outlaws began to look round for fresh interests. They were torn between a desire to return to the woods and fields that were the usual scenes of their activities and a feeling that to leave house and garden of Ginger's home in the present circumstances was to waste a golden opportunity that might never occur again.

For Aunt Arabelle, shut in the library, writing her Answers to Correspondents and articles on How to Beautify the Home or Feed the Husband or Renovate the Wardrobe on a Small Income, remained blind and deaf to all their doings and the domestic staff of Ginger's home had long since washed its hands of him.

'Let's think of something *really* exciting to do,' said William.

It was Ginger who thought of it.

'Let's have a sea fight in the conservatory with paper boats an' sticks to guide 'em,' he said. 'We can turn on the tap enough to have the floor jus' underwater, an' the floor's made of tiles so it won't do it any harm, an' we won't have enough to go up the step into the hall.'

The idea was adopted eagerly by the Outlaws and

they set to work at once making fleets of paper boats. Then they flooded the conservatory. They found that as the 'sea' trickled out beneath the door into the garden it was necessary to replenish it at frequent intervals. It was Ginger's idea to leave the tap on, 'Just enough to keep a decent sea,' and in the excitement of the ensuing naval conflict they did not notice that the tap had been left on too full and that the water was rising above the step into the hall.

Aunt Arabelle, a far-away smile on her lips (she had just written a very beautiful little article on the Art of the Love Letter), stepped from the study to the hall and was brought down to earth abruptly by finding herself standing in a large pool of water. It struck cold and clammy through the moccasins that she always wore when she was working. It swirled around her ankles. Aunt Arabelle clutched her skirts about her in terror and, without stopping to consider the particular element that was threatening her, shouted: 'Fire!' The cook rushed out from the kitchen with the fire extinguisher and as she had completely lost her head and as Aunt Arabelle was still shouting: 'Fire,' proceeded to drench Aunt Arabelle with its contents.

The Outlaws heard the commotion and hastily turned off the tap. But it was too late. Aunt Arabelle had been roughly shaken out of the hazy vagueness in which she usually lived. Some of the contents of the fire extinguisher had gone into her mouth and the taste was not pleasant. The apple-green smock in which she always worked was ruined. In short, the 'absolute crisis' had arrived in which she had decreed that she and Ginger should trouble each other.

'I can't *possibly* tell your mother you've been good now,' she said to Ginger.

The Outlaws, who in the intervals of devising the new games, had planned the spending of Ginger's good conduct money to the last farthing – and had even spent some of it on credit at the local sweetshop – were aghast. They used their utmost powers of persuasion on Aunt Arabelle but in vain. 'I can't possibly,' said Aunt Arabelle simply. 'I'd be telling an untruth if I said that Ginger had been good and I couldn't *possibly* tell an untruth.'

It was a point of view from which they found it impossible to shake her. Gloom descended upon them. Even the house had lost its charms. They walked down into the village, carefully avoiding the local sweetshop. And in the village they met Anthony Martin. They did not know that he was Anthony Martin, of course. They saw a little boy of about six, picturesquely attired, wearing a complacent expression and hair that was just too long. He was a stranger to the locality.

'Who are you?' said William.

'Don't you know?' said the little boy with a self-conscious smile. 'I'm Anthony Martin.'

William's face remained blank. The little boy seemed disappointed by their reception of the information. 'Don't you know Anthony Martin?' he said.

'No. Never heard of him,' said Ginger.

A shade of contempt came into the little boy's face.

'Good heavens!' he said. 'Whatever sort of books do you read?'

'Pirates an' Red Indian stories,' said William.

The boy looked pained and disgusted.

'Good *heavens!*' he said again. 'I shouldn't have thought there was *anyone* ... Haven't you read any of the Anthony Martin books?'

'No,' said William, unimpressed. 'Did you write 'em? I've written books myself.'

'No, my mother writes them, but they're about me. Poems and stories. All about me. Nearly half a million copies have been sold and they've been translated into fourteen different languages. I've had my photograph in literally hundreds of papers. *Good* papers, I mean. Not rubbish. They're *literary* stories and poems, you know. Really cultured people buy them for their children. There were several Anthony Martin parties in London last year. *Hundreds* of children came. Just to see me. Have you *really* never heard of me?'

William had never met anyone like this before and he was for the time being too much taken aback to do himself justice. He merely gasped, 'No ... never.'

'You can't know much about *books*, then,' went on the child scornfully, 'and your people can't either, or they'd have bought them for you. They're *the* children's classic nowadays. I have *hundreds* of letters from people who've read them. People I've never met. They send me presents at Christmas, too. And ...'

'Why have you come here?' said William, stemming the flood.

'My mother's come for a rest,' said Anthony Martin, 'she's been overworking. And people have been rushing us so. I've got *sick* of Anthony Martin parties. But it seems unkind to disappoint people and they do so love to see me. We're going to spend a very quiet fortnight down here. I'm not going to give any interviews. Except perhaps one. The editor of *The Helicon* wants to send someone down and I've half promised to be photographed on her knee. Of course, I don't *quite* know whether I shall yet. Well, I must go home to lunch now. Tell your people you've seen me. They'll be

**35**

interested. I simply can't understand your never having heard of me. Good morning.'

The Outlaws stood open-mouthed and watched Anthony Martin's small, dapper figure as it strolled nonchalantly away.

Then they turned gloomily homeward. The incident had increased their depression. They found Aunt Arabelle dried and changed and in a state of great excitement.

'My dears,' she said, 'you'll never *guess* who's come to stay in the village. Anthony Martin!'

'We've seen him,' said William dejectedly.

'But, my dears, aren't you *thrilled?*'

'No,' said William.

'You know his *sweet* things, don't you?'

'No,' said William.

'Oh, I must read some to you. I've got them nearly all here. I never go anywhere without them.'

The dejection of the Outlaws deepened still more.

'You've actually *seen* him?' went on Aunt Arabelle eagerly.

'Yes.'

'Oh, my dears, I *must* see him. I wonder ... No, I suppose it would be *impossible* ...'

'What?' said Ginger.

'I have written several times officially and I've had

no answer. Of course the *Woman's Sphere* isn't *quite* ...
I mean they can't be *expected* ... but he does give
interviews quite a lot.'

'Oh, yes,' said Ginger, 'he said he was doing that.
Being photographed on someone's knee.'

'Oh, *lucky* someone!' said Aunt Arabelle ecstatically.
'Did he say what paper?'

'Sounded like a pelican,' said William.

'*The Helicon*,' said Aunt Arabelle humbly. 'Ah, yes,
of course ...' and she sighed deeply, wistfully.

William looked at her and the ghost of the lost ten
shillings glimmered faintly on his mental horizon.

'Do you want him to interview you very much?'
he said.

'The other way round, dear boy. I want him to grant
*me* an interview with *him*. More than anything else in
the world.'

'Do you know where he's staying?' said William.

'I heard that they'd taken Honeysuckle Cottage,' said
Aunt Arabelle. 'I must try to get a *peep* at him anyway.'

When Anthony Martin strolled out into the garden
of Honeysuckle Cottage after tea, he found the four
Outlaws standing in a row at the gate. Anthony Martin
was accustomed to people hanging about to catch a
glimpse of him and took it as his right, but the

Outlaws' ignorance had piqued his vanity. He strolled up to them slowly.

'I simply can't make out how you've never come across those books,' he said. 'They're *everywhere*. All the bookshops are full of them. There was my photograph in nearly all the bookshops last Christmas. And there was an Anthony Martin Christmas card. Why, I could go out to tea every day of the year if I wanted to.'

'Look here,' said William, making himself the spokesman, 'will you give an interview to Ginger's aunt? It's a *very* important paper.'

'We'll let you play Red Indians with us if you will,' said Ginger.

'We'll show you the best place for fishing,' said Henry.

'We'll take you to our secret place in the woods,' said Douglas.

'Good *heavens!*' said Anthony Martin contemptuously. 'That sort of thing doesn't appeal to me in the *least* ... What is the paper?'

'It's called *The Woman Spear*,' said Ginger.

'Never heard of it. What sort of thing does it go in for?'

'Dumbness and stomach-ache and heart disease and things like that,' said William.

'I've never given an interview to a medical paper before,' said Anthony Martin importantly. 'Look here – our agent's coming over to see us tomorrow. I'll ask him. He knows all about these papers. Come here this time tomorrow and I'll let you know.'

So high had the hopes of the Outlaws risen in the interval that by the time they assembled at the gate of Honeysuckle Cottage the next evening they had borrowed sixpence from Victor Jameson on the strength of the ten shillings and made new and revised arrangements for the expenditure of the rest.

The small and picturesque figure swaggered down to them through the dusk.

'Well?' said Ginger eagerly.

'It's a jolly good paper,' said William, 'it's got better stuff on dumbness and stomach-ache and heart disease than any other paper going.'

'We'll give you sixpence of it,' said Henry, referring to the ten shillings and forgetting that Anthony Martin didn't know about it.

We'll show you a robin's nest,' said Douglas.

Anthony Martin dismissed the whole subject with a wave of his hand.

'It's absolutely off,' he said. 'Our agent says that it's a piffling paper and that I mustn't on *any* account give an interview to it. It hasn't even any circulation to speak of.'

'It does speak of circulation,' said William, pugnaciously, 'it's included in heart disease.'

'You don't know what you're talking about,' said Anthony Martin loftily. 'Our agent says it isn't a medical paper at all. It's a twopenny-halfpenny rag.'

'It wouldn't do you any harm jus' to give her an interview,' pleaded Ginger.

'My dear boy, it would,' said Anthony Martin. 'It would cheapen our market and that's the last thing we want to do ... Anyway, my mother said you could come to tea tomorrow if you liked.'

'Thanks awfully,' said William with a fairly good imitation of politeness.

'I want to show you some of our Press cuttings,' said Anthony Martin.

It was clear that he felt a true missionary zeal to convert them to his cult.

'Don't bring your aunt,' he warned them, 'because I shan't see her. And it's no use your telling her things I say because she can't use them without our permission.'

The next day, the Outlaws presented themselves, clean and tidy, at Honeysuckle Cottage. They were first of all taken to Anthony Martin's mother, who lay on a sofa in the front room with the blinds down, garbed in an elaborate rest gown, her head swathed in a sort of turban. She raised a limp hand in protest as they entered.

'On tiptoe, please, boys. Every sound goes through my head. I'm always like this between the visits of my creative genius. Prostrated. No one knows what I suffer ...' The limp hand raised a pair of lorgnettes[3] from among the folds of the elaborate rest gown and she surveyed the four in silence for several moments. The result of her inspection seemed to deepen her gloom. 'How *sweet* of him to ask you,' was her final comment. 'I hope you realize that hundreds of people would give almost *anything* for the privilege. I hope you will remember this afternoon all your lives ...' The limp hand dismissed them with an airy wave, then went to her suffering head as the Outlaws clumped their way out.

Upstairs, Anthony Martin had a suite all to himself, consisting of a small sitting room, a small drawing room and a small bedroom. This self-contained kingdom was presided over by a crushed-looking creature in a cap and apron whom Anthony Martin addressed as 'Nurse' and treated with the hauteur of an Oriental despot.

'I want you to hear my latest record first,' he said to his guests. 'Mother's having records made of the

---

[3] Spectacles with a long handle.

Anthony Martin poems recited by me. She's going to give four very select Anthony Martin parties when we get back to London and she's having the records made for that. They're not being issued to the public yet. This is "Homework". It's a very popular one. Every verse ends with "Anthony Martin is doing his sums".'

He put on the record and the Outlaws listened to it in a dejected silence.

'I'm making another one tomorrow,' went on Anthony Martin when it was finished. 'A man's coming in from Hadley with the thing, and I recite into it and then they make the record from the impression. I'm going to do "Walking in the Puddles" tomorrow. Mother likes me to be quite alone with her when I recite them for records. Anyone else in the room disturbs the atmosphere.'

He took down a large album and gave it to William.

'You can look at the Press cuttings and I'll take the others into my bedroom and show them the toys that come in the stories. You can go downstairs and fetch up the tea now, Nurse.'

William was left alone in the little sitting room with the album of Press cuttings. He turned the pages over idly.

Suddenly the door opened and a man entered carrying a kind of gramophone.

'As the front door was open,' he said, 'I came straight up with this 'ere. It wasn't wanted till tomorrow, but as I was over with something for the Vicarage I thought I'd leave it.'

He looked at William in surprise.

'You aren't the young gent, are you?'

'No,' said William hastily, 'he's in his bedroom.'

'Well, never mind botherin' him,' said the man, 'jus' tell 'im I've brought it. I'll explain 'ow it works in case they've forgotten. It's all ready for takin' the impression an' all they have to do is pull out this 'ere and that lets the sound through to the wax. Then take out the finished impression –'ere – and bring it down to us an' we'll fix it up.' He looked round the room and finally set down the instrument behind a small settee. 'That's nice an' out of the way till they want it tomorrow, isn't it?'

Then he creaked downstairs and out of the open front door leaving William gloomily turning over the pages of the album. The crushed-looking nurse brought up tea and the six of them took their places round the table. Anthony Martin alone sustained the conversation. He had still a lot to tell his new friends, still a lot to show them. He had a letter signed by a royal personage. He had a present sent to him by the wife of a cabinet minister. He had a photograph of himself taken with an eminent literary celebrity. The

**43**

crushed-looking nurse interrupted this monologue to say:

'Now drink up your milk, Master Anthony.'

'Shan't,' returned the world-famous infant.

'You know the doctor told your mother you'd got to drink a glass of milk every teatime.'

'You shut up,' said the winsome child.

'Your mother said I wasn't to let you get up from tea till you'd had it,' said the nurse.

Anthony Martin turned on her with a torrent of invective which showed that, as far as mastery over words and their fitness for the occasion was concerned, he had inherited much of his mother's literary talent.

During it William remembered that he had forgotten to tell them about the man with the gramophone. Then a sudden light seemed to shine from his face. He slipped from the room and returned in a few minutes, leaving the door ajar, ostentatiously flourishing his handkerchief and muttering:

'Sorry, left it in there.' Anthony Martin proceeded undisturbed with his 'scene', his voice upraised shrilly:

'Shan't drink it up ... All right, you try to make me, you old hag. I'll throw it in your nasty old face. I'll kick your nasty old shins. I'll stamp on your nasty old toes. You leave me alone, I tell you, you old cat, you! I'll tell my mother. Do you think I'm going to do what you tell me now I'm famous all over the world? I …'

It went on for five or ten minutes. William sat listening with a smile on his face that puzzled the others. It ended by Anthony Martin's not drinking his milk and the depressed nurse feebly threatening to tell his mother when she felt better.

After tea William asked if he might still go on reading the press cuttings and if Ginger might look at them with him as he was sure that Ginger would enjoy them. Anthony Martin also was sure that Ginger would enjoy them. 'I'll leave you to read them here,' he said, 'and I'll finish showing the other two the things in my bedroom and then they can read the cuttings and I'll show you the things upstairs.'

The other Outlaws were still more puzzled by William's attitude. They felt that he was pandering to this atrocious child without getting them anywhere. They followed his lead as ever, though in a reluctant hangdog fashion that was small tribute to Anthony Martin's much paragraphed 'charm'.

Douglas and Henry followed him gloomily into the little bedroom that partook of the nature of an Anthony Martin museum (Anthony Martin's mother took the stage properties with them even on short visits), leaving Ginger and William sitting side by side on the little settee, their heads bent over the album of Press cuttings. As soon as the door had closed on them, William sprang up, dived behind the settee and emerged with something that he held beneath his coat.

'When he comes down tell him I don't feel well and I've gone home,' he said and slipped from the room, leaving Ginger mystified but cheered, for it was evident that William's fertile brain had evolved a plan.

The man at the gramophone shop down in Hadley received him and his precious burden without suspicion.

'Oh, yes,' he said, 'tell them I'll have it ready first thing tomorrow. You'll call for it? Very good. An honour for the neighbourhood to have the little gentleman here, isn't it?' William agreed without enthusiasm and departed.

He was at the gramophone shop early the next morning. He looked rather anxious and his posture as he entered the shop suggested the posture of one prepared for instant flight. But evidently nothing had happened in the meantime to give him away. The gramophone man was depressed but not suspicious.

'I think it's a mistake,' he said, as he handed the record over to William. 'It's quite out of his usual line and personally I don't think it'll be popular. It's not the sort of thing the public cares for.'

William seized his parcel and escaped. At the end

of the street he met the crushed-looking nurse. She recognized him and stopped.

'Where's the gramophone shop?' she said.

William, still poised for flight, pointed it out to her.

'They sent the thing up,' she complained, 'a day before we asked for it an' without leavin' no word an' without the proper thing in. We've only jus' come across it behind the settee. An' there's no telephone in the house so I've got to traipse down here. Would you like to come back with me and carry it up?'

'I'm frightfully sorry,' said William, 'but I'm very busy this morning.'

He just caught the bus from Hadley. There wasn't another one for half an hour. That gave him half an hour's start. Aunt Arabelle had gone out for the morning constitutional (she called it 'communing with Nature') that gave her the necessary inspiration for her day's work. The Outlaws were waiting for him at Ginger's gate and accompanied him at a run to Honeysuckle Cottage. Anthony Martin was strolling aimlessly and sulkily about the garden.

'Hallo,' he said; then to William, 'Are you better?'

'Yes, thanks,' said William.

'I expect you aren't used to such a good tea as you got yesterday,' said Anthony Martin and added morbidly, 'I'm sick of the country. There's nothing to do in it. It's all very well for writing poems about, but it's rotten to stay in. Mother made up a ripping one last night called: "Staying in the Country". Every verse ends "Anthony Martin is milking a cow". She's prostrated again today, of course.'

'Will you come over to Ginger's house?' said William. 'We've got something to show you there.'

The disgust on Anthony Martin's face deepened.

'It's likely *you'd* have anything I'd want to see,' he said. 'It's your aunt wants to see me, an' I'm jolly well not going to let her.'

'No, she's out,' said Ginger, 'an' it's something you'll be jolly interested in.'

'Is it about *me*?' said Anthony Martin.

'Yes,' said Ginger.

Anthony Martin shrugged petulantly.

'I'm always being shown things in the papers about myself that I ought to have seen first,' he said, 'the press cutting agencies are so abominably slack.' He threw a bored glance round the garden. 'Well, I may as well come as stay here, I suppose, as long as your aunt isn't there.'

It was a relief to have secured him before the crushed-looking nurse arrived back with her sensational news.

Anthony Martin accompanied them to Ginger's house, giving them as they went his frank views on the country and the people who lived in it. They received his views in silence.

'Well, what is it?' he said as he entered the house.

'It's a gramophone record,' said William.

'Something of mine?'

'Yes.'

'My dear fellow, it's not recited by me, because none of them are issued yet. A good many of my things *are* done on records, I know, but not recited by me and that makes all the difference. Fancy bringing me all this way just for that!'

'It's one you've not heard,' said Ginger.

'I bet it isn't. I've heard them all.'

'All right. We'll put it on and you can see.'

He followed them into the morning-room, where a gramophone stood on a table by the window. In silence, William put a record on. There came a grating sound, then a shrill voice tempestuously upraised:

'Shan't drink it up. All right, you *try* to make me, you old hag. I'll throw it in your nasty old face. I'll kick your nasty old shins. I'll stamp on your nasty old toes. You leave me alone, I tell you, you old cat, you! I'll tell my mother. D'you think I'm going to do what you tell me when I'm famous all over the world ...'

There was, of course, a lot more in the same strain.

Though not the sweet, flutelike voice of the record 'Homework', it was unmistakably Anthony Martin's voice. Anthony Martin's aplomb dropped from him. He turned a dull, beet red. His eyes protruded with anger and horror. His mouth hung open.

He made a sudden spring towards the gramophone, but Ginger and Henry caught him and held him in an iron grip while Douglas took off the record and William put it in a cupboard, locked it and pocketed the key.

'Now what are you going to do?' said William.

The result was a continuation of the record with some picturesque additions.

'It's no use going on like that,' said William sternly. 'We've got it and everyone'll know it's you all right even if they've never heard you go on like that.'

'It's illegal,' screamed Anthony Martin. 'I'll go to the police about it. It's stealing.'

'All right, go to the police,' said William. 'I'll hide it where neither the police nor anyone else can find it. And I'll take jolly good care that a lot of people hear it. Ginger's aunt's having a party here this afternoon and they'll hear it first thing. I bet that in a week everyone'll know about it.'

Anthony Martin burst into angry sobs. He stamped and kicked and bit and scratched, but Ginger and

Henry continued to hold him in the iron grip.

'Now, listen to us,' said William at last. 'This is the only record and we'll give it to you so that you can break it up or throw it away on one condition.'

'What's that?' said Anthony Martin checking his sobs to listen.

'That you give Ginger's aunt an interview for her paper and have your photograph taken sitting on her knee same as you were going to for the other.'

There was a long silence during which Anthony Martin wrestled with his professional pride. Finally he gulped, spluttered and said, 'All right, you beasts. Give it to me.'

'When you've given my aunt the interview,' said Ginger.

When Ginger's aunt returned, Ginger met her on the doorstep.

'He's here,' he said, 'and he's going to give you an interview for your paper. And he'll have his photograph taken on your knee. He's rung up the photographer in Hadley to do it and he'll be here any time now.'

All the rest of that day Aunt Arabelle had to keep pinching herself to make sure that she was awake.

'My dears, it's too *wonderful* to be true. So *sweet*, isn't he? Such a *lesson* to all you boys. The things he said in the interview brought tears to my eyes. I only wish you boys loved beauty as that little child does. It's a wonderful interview. The editress will simply die of joy when she gets it.'

William fixed her with a stony gaze.

'We took a jolly lot of trouble getting him to give it to you.'

'I'm sure you did, dear boys,' said Aunt Arabelle, 'and I'm *so* grateful.'

'That tap that Ginger left on by mistake ...'

There was a long silence during which William and Aunt Arabelle looked at each other and the connection between the tap and the interview dawned gradually upon Aunt Arabelle's simple mind. Her eyes slid away from William's.

'Well, of course,' she said, 'when one comes to think of it, no actual *harm* was done. In fact, *really* it was no more than – than just washing out the floor of the conservatory and hall. No, Ginger dear, on thinking the matter over, I see nothing in that episode to justify me in making any complaints to your parents.'

Aunt Arabelle stayed for the night of Ginger's parents' return. Ginger's parents were inordinately, as Ginger considered, full of their travels and described them at what Ginger thought undue length. Even Aunt Arabelle grew restive. Finally Ginger's mother noticed the restiveness and said kindly, 'And have you any news, dear?'

With sparkling eyes and flushed cheeks Aunt Arabelle poured out her news in a turgid stream.

'Anthony Martin, you know ... *the* Anthony Martin ... yes, *here* ... a *whole* half-hour's interview ... and the editress was so pleased that she paid me double my usual terms, and she's going to give me all the important interviews now and she's raised my rate of payment for all my work.'

'How splendid,' said Ginger's mother. 'And has Ginger been good?'

The eyes of Ginger and Aunt Arabelle met in a glance of complete understanding.

'*Perfectly* good,' said Aunt Arabelle. '*Quite* a help, in fact.'

'I'm so glad,' said Ginger's mother.

'You said ten shillings,' Ginger reminded her casually.

She took a ten shilling note out of her purse and handed it to him.

'And now, Ginger dear,' she went on, 'I want to tell you about some more of the wonderful cathedrals we've seen.'

But Ginger had already slipped out to join the Outlaws, who were waiting for him at the garden gate.

# The Eyes Have It

## by Philip K. Dick

It was quite by accident I discovered this incredible invasion of Earth by lifeforms from another planet. As yet, I haven't done anything about it; I can't think of anything to do. I wrote to the Government and they sent back a pamphlet on the repair and maintenance of frame houses. Anyhow, the whole thing is known; I'm not the first to discover it. Maybe it's even under control.

I was sitting in my easy-chair, idly turning the pages of a paperbacked book someone had left on the bus, when I came across the reference that first put me on the trail. For a moment I didn't respond. It took some time for the full import to sink in. After I'd comprehended, it seemed odd I hadn't noticed it right away.

The reference was clearly to a nonhuman species of incredible properties, not indigenous to Earth. A species, I hasten to point out, customarily masquerading as ordinary human beings. Their disguise, however, became transparent in the face of the following observations by the author. It was at once obvious the author knew everything.

Knew everything – and was taking it in his stride. The line (and I tremble remembering it even now) read:

*... his eyes slowly roved about the room.*

Vague chills assailed me. I tried to picture the eyes. Did they roll like dimes? The passage indicated not; they seemed to move through the air, not over the surface. Rather rapidly, apparently. No one in the story was surprised. That's what tipped me off. No sign of amazement at such an outrageous thing. Later the matter was amplified.

*... his eyes moved from person to person.*

There it was in a nutshell. The eyes had clearly come apart from the rest of him and were on their own. My heart pounded and my breath choked in my windpipe. I had stumbled on an accidental mention of a totally unfamiliar race. Obviously non-terrestrial. Yet, to the characters in the book, it was perfectly natural – which suggested they belonged to the same species.

And the author? A slow suspicion burned in my mind. The author was taking it rather *too easily* in his stride. Evidently, he felt this was quite a usual thing. He made absolutely no attempt to conceal this knowledge. The story continued:

*... presently his eyes fastened on Julia.*

Julia, being a lady, had at least the breeding to feel indignant. She is described as blushing and knitting her brows angrily. At this, I sighed with relief. They weren't *all* non-terrestrials. The narrative continues:

*... slowly, calmly, his eyes examined every inch of her.*

Great Scott! But here the girl turned and stomped off and the matter ended. I lay back in my chair gasping with horror. My wife and family regarded me in wonder.

'What's wrong, dear?' my wife asked.

I couldn't tell her. Knowledge like this was too much for the ordinary run-of-the-mill person. I had to keep it to myself. 'Nothing,' I gasped. I leaped up, snatched the book and hurried out of the room.

In the garage, I continued reading. There was more. Trembling, I read the next revealing passage:

*... he put his arm around Julia. Presently she asked him if he would remove his arm. He immediately did so, with a smile.*

It's not said what was done with the arm after the fellow had removed it. Maybe it was left standing upright in the corner. Maybe it was thrown away. I don't care. In any case, the full meaning was there, staring me right in the face.

Here was a race of creatures capable of removing portions of their anatomy at will. Eyes, arms – and maybe more. Without batting an eyelash. My knowledge of biology came in handy, at this point. Obviously they were simple beings, uni-cellular, some sort of primitive single-celled things. Beings no more developed than starfish. Starfish can do the same thing, you know.

I read on. And came to this incredible revelation, tossed off coolly by the author without the faintest tremor:

*... outside the movie theater we split up. Part of us went inside, part over to the cafe for dinner.*

Binary fission, obviously. Splitting in half and forming two entities. Probably each lower half went to the cafe, it being farther and the upper halves to the movies. I read on, hands shaking. I had really stumbled onto something here. My mind reeled as I made out this passage:

*... I'm afraid there's no doubt about it. Poor Bibney has lost his head again.*

Which was followed by:

*... and Bob says he has utterly no guts.*

Yet Bibney got around as well as the next person. The next person, however, was just as strange. He was soon described as:

*... totally lacking in brains.*

There was no doubt of the thing in the next passage. Julia, whom I had thought to be the one normal person, reveals herself as also being an alien lifeform, similar to the rest:

*... quite deliberately, Julia had given her heart to the young man.*

It didn't relate what the final disposition of the organ was, but I didn't really care. It was evident Julia had gone right on living in her usual manner, like all the others in the book. Without heart, arms, eyes, brains, viscera, dividing up in two when the occasion demanded. Without a qualm.

*... thereupon she gave him her hand.*

I sickened. The rascal now had her hand, as well as her heart. I shudder to think what he's done with them, by this time.

*... he took her arm.*

Not content to wait, he had to start dismantling her on his own. Flushing crimson, I slammed the book shut and leaped to my feet. But not in time to escape one last reference to those carefree bits of anatomy whose travels had originally thrown me on the track:

*... her eyes followed him all the way down the road and across the meadow.*

I rushed from the garage and back inside the warm house, as if the accursed things were following *me*. My wife and children were playing Monopoly in the kitchen. I joined them and played with frantic fervour, brow feverish, teeth chattering.

I had had enough of the thing. I want to hear no more about it. Let them come on. Let them invade Earth. I don't want to get mixed up in it. I have absolutely no stomach for it.

# Tom Tit Tot

## by Alan Garner

Well, once upon a time, there was a woman and she baked five pies. And when they came out of the oven, they were that overbaked, the crust was too hard to eat. So she said to her daughter, 'Put them pies on the shelf,' she said, 'and leave them a little and they'll come again.' She meant, you know, that the crust would get soft.

But the girl, she said to herself, 'If they'll come again, I'll eat them now.' And she set to work and ate them all, first and last.

Well, come supper time, the woman she said, 'Go you and get one of them there pies. I daresay they've come again now.'

The girl she went and she looked and there wasn't nothing but the dishes. So back she came and said she, 'No, they ain't come again.'

'Not none of them?' said the mother.

'Not none of them,' said she.

'Well, come again or not come again,' said the woman, 'I'll have one for supper.'

'But you can't if they ain't come,' said the girl.

'But I can,' said she. 'Go you and bring the best of them.'

'Best or worst,' said the girl, 'I've ate them all and you can't have one till it's come again.'

Well, the woman she was wholly bate[1] and she took her spinning to the door, to spin and as she spun she sang:

'My daughter ate five, five pies today;
My daughter ate five, five pies today.'

The king was coming down the street and he heard her sing, but what she sang he couldn't hear, so he stopped and said, 'What was that you were singing of?'

The woman she was ashamed to let him hear what her daughter had been doing, so she sang instead of that:

'My daughter spun five, five skeins[2] today;
My daughter spun five, five skeins today.'

'Stars of mine!' said the king. 'I never heard tell of anyone who could do that.'

Then he said, 'Look you here, I want a wife and I'll marry your daughter. But look you here,' said he, 'eleven months out of twelve she shall have all the vittles[3] she likes to eat and all the gowns she likes to get, and all the company she likes to keep; but the last

---

[1] Angry.
[2] A ball of yarn.
[3] Food.

month of the year she'll have to spin five skeins every day and if she doesn't, I shall kill her.'

'All right,' said the woman; for she thought that was a grand marriage, that was. And as for them five skeins, when it came to, there'd be plenty of ways of getting out of it and likeliest he'd have forgotten about it.

Well, so they married. And for eleven months the girl had all the vittles she liked to eat and all the gowns she liked to get and all the company she liked to keep.

But when the time was getting over, she began to think about them there skeins and to wonder if he had them in mind. But not one word did he say about them and she wholly thought he'd forgotten.

However, the last day of the eleventh month, he took her to a room she'd never set eyes on before. There was nothing in it but a spinning wheel and a stool.

And said he, 'Now, my dear, here you'll be shut in tomorrow, with some vittles and some flax[4] and if you haven't spun five skeins by the night, your head'll go off.'

And away he went about his business.

Well, she was that frightened. She'd always been such a heedless girl that she didn't so much as know how to spin and what was she to do tomorrow with no one to come near to help her? She sat down on a stool

---

[4] The stalk of a plant that can be spun into yarn.

in the kitchen and lork! How she did cry!

However, all on a sudden, she heard a sort of knocking low down on the door. She cupped and opened it and what should she see but a small little black thing with a long tail. It looked up at her right curious and it said, 'What are you crying for?'

'What's that to you?' said she.

'Never you mind,' it said, 'but tell me what you're crying for.'

'It don't do me no good if I do,' said she.

'You don't know that,' it said and twirled its tail round.

'Well,' said she, 'it won't do no harm, if it don't do no good,' and she upped and told about the pies and the skeins and everything.

'This is what I'll do,' said the little black thing. 'I'll come to your window every morning and take the flax and bring it spun at night.'

'What's your pay?' said she.

It looked out of the corners of its eyes, and it said, 'I'll give you three guesses every night to guess my name; and if you haven't guessed it before the month's up, you shall be mine.'

Well, she thought she'd be sure to guess its name before the month was up. 'All right,' said she. 'I agree.'

'All right,' it said and lork! How it twirled its tail.

The next day her husband he took her into the room and there was the flax and the day's vittles.

'Now there's the flax,' said he. 'And if that ain't spun up this night, off goes your head.' And then he went out and locked the door.

He'd hardly gone, when there was a knocking against the window. She opened it and there, sure enough, was the little old thing sitting on the ledge.

'Where's the flax?' it said.

'Here it be,' said she. And she gave it to him.

Well, come the evening, a knocking fell again on the window. She opened it and there was the little old thing, with five skeins of flax on its arm.

'Here it be,' it said and it gave the flax to the girl. 'Now, what's my name?'

'What, is it Bill?' said she.

'No, it ain't,' it said and it twirled its tail.

'Is it Ned?' said she.

'No, it ain't,' it said, and it twirled its tail.

'Is it Dick?' said she.

'No, it ain't,' it said. And it twirled its tail harder, and away it flew.

Well, when the husband he came in, there were the five skeins ready for him.

'I see I shan't have to kill you tonight, my dear,' said he. 'You'll have your vittles and your flax in the morning,' said he and away he went.

Well, every day the flax and the vittles, they were brought and every day that there little black impet[5] used to come mornings and evenings.

And all the day the girl she sat trying to think of names to say to it when it came at night, but she never hit on the right one. And as it got towards the end of the month, the impet[5] it began to look so maliceful and it twirled its tail faster and faster each time she gave a guess.

It came to the last day but one. The impet it came at night along with the five skeins and it said, 'What, ain't you got my name yet?'

'Is it Rob?' said she.

'No, it ain't,' it said.

'Is it Hob?' said she.

'No, it ain't,' it said.

'Is it Lob?' said she.

'No, it ain't that neither,' it said.

Then it looked at her with its eyes like a coal of fire and it said, 'Woman, there's only tomorrow night and then you'll be mine.' And away it flew.

Well, she felt that horrid. However, she heard the

---

[5] A malevolent sprite.

king coming along the passage.

In he came and when he saw the five skeins, he said, said he, 'Well, my dear, I don't see but what you'll have your skeins ready tomorrow night as well and as I reckon I shan't have to kill you, I'll have supper in here tonight.'

So they brought supper and another stool for him, and down the two they sat.

Now he hadn't eaten but a mouthful or so, when he stopped and began to laugh.

'What is it?' said she.

'Why,' said he, 'I was out hunting today and I got away to a place in the wood I'd never seen before. There was an old chalk pit. And I heard a sort of humming, kind of. So I got off my hobby[6] and I went right quiet to the pit, and I looked down. Well, what should there be but the funniest little black thing you ever set eyes on. And what was that doing but it had a little spinning wheel, and it was spinning wonderful fast, and twirling its tail. And as it spun, it sang:

"Nimmy nimmy not,
My name's Tom Tit Tot!"'

Well, when the girl heard this, she fared as if she could have jumped out of her skin for joy; but she

---

[6] A horse.

didn't say a word.

Next day, that there little thing looked so maliceful when it came for the flax. And at night, she heard it knocking against the window panes. She opened the window and it came right in on the ledge. It was grinning from ear to ear, and oh! Its tail was twirling round so fast.

'What's my name?' it said as it gave her the skeins.

'Is it Bullbeggar?' said she, pretending to be afraid.

'No, it ain't,' it said, and it came further into the room.

'Is it Clabbernapper?' said she.

'No, it ain't,' said the impet. And then it laughed and twirled its tail till you couldn't hardly see it. 'Take time, woman,' it said. 'Next guess and you're mine!' And it stretched out its black hands to her.

She backed a step or two, and she looked at it, and then she laughed out, and said she, pointing of her finger at it:

'Nimmy nimmy not,
Your name's Tom Tit Tot!'

Well, when it heard her, it shruk awful, and away it flew, into the dark and she never saw it no more.

# The Molesworth Self-Adjusting Thank-You Letter

## by Geoffrey Willans and Ronald Searle

As an after xmas wheeze n. molesworth presents his
self - adjusting thank-you letter.

Cut out hours of toil pen biting wear on elbows,
blotches and staring out of windows.

Strike Out words which do not apply.

| Dear { | Aunt |
|--------|------|
| | Uncle |
| | Stinker |
| | Gran |
| | Clot |
| | Pen-Pal |

| Thank you very much for the { | train. tractor. germ gun. kite. delicious present.* sweets. space pistol. toy socks. |
|-------------------------------|------------------------------------------------------------------------------------|
| It was { | lovely. useful. just as good as the other three. not bad. super. |

* When you can't remember what it was.

68

| And I have | { | played with it constantly.<br>bust it already.<br>no patience with it.<br>given it to the poor boys.<br>dismantled it. |
| --- | --- | --- |

| I am feeling | { | very well.<br>very poorly.<br>lousy.<br>in tip-top form.<br>sick. | } | I hope you<br>are too. |
| --- | --- | --- | --- | --- |

My birthday when next present is due is on _____

From _____

*(Postage must be prepaid.)*

# Music the Food of Luv

## by Geoffrey Willans and Ronald Searle

Sooner or later yore parents decide that they ought to give you a chance to hav a bash at the piano. So wot hapen, eh ? They go up to GRIMES, headmaster, who is dealing in his inimitable way, my dere, with a number of problems from other parents, e.g. fotherington-tomas' vests, peasons cough drops, grabber's gold pen and pore, pore mrs gillibrand thinks that ian (who is so sensitive) is the tiniest bit unhappy about the condukt of sigismund the mad maths master. (Who wouldn't be? He is utterly bats and more crooked than the angle A.) Finally come the turn of those super, smashing and cultured family hem-hem the molesworths. Mum step forward britely:

Oh, mr GRIMES, she sa, we think it would be so nice for nigel and his wee bro, molesworth 2, to learn the piano this term.

(GRIMES thinks: Another mug. One born every minit.)

GRIMES: Yes, yes, mrs molesworth, i think we could manage to squeeze them in. Judging from their drawings both yore sons hav strong artistick tendencies, i see them in their later years drawing solace from bach and beethoven ect in some cloistered drawing room. It'll cost you ten nicker and not a penny less.

PATER: (*feebly*) I sa—

GRIMES: Look at the wear and tear on the piano – it's a bektenstein, you kno. Then there's the metronome – had to have new sparking plugs last hols and the time is coming when we've got to hav a new pianoforte tutor.

*Pater and Mater weakly agree and the old GRIMES cash register ring merily out again. It is in this way that that grate genius of the keyboard, molesworth 2, learned to pla that grate piece fairy bells chiz chiz chiz.*

The first thing when you learn to pla the piano is to stare out of the window for 20 minits with yore mouth open. Then scratch yore head and carve yore name, adding it to the illustrious list already inscribed on the top of the piano. Should, however, GRIMES or any of the other beaks becom aware that there is no sound of mery musick, the pupil should pretend to be studdying the KEYBOARD in his instruktion book.

This is meant to teach the eager pupil the names of

the notes ect. The skool piano may hav looked like that once, but toda it is very different. Before getting on to rimski-korsakov it is as well to kno wot you are up aganst. Here is the guide –

C – this one go plunk.

D – the top hav come off the note and you strike melody from something like a cheese ringer.

E – sticks down when you hit it. Bring yore screwdriver to lever it up.

F – have never been the same since molesworth 2 put his chewing gum under it.

G – nothing hapen when you hit this note at all.

Do not be discouraged, however, show grit, courage, determination, concentrate, attend and soon you will get yoreself a piece. This will probably be called Happy Thorts and there is a strong warning at the beginning which sa Not Too Fast. Who do they think i am, eh, Stirling Moss?

# Never Trust a Parrot

## by Jeremy Strong

*Dear Pet Problem Page,*
*You are my last chance of hope. I pray that you can help*
*me. I have a problem with my parrot. I had better start at*
*the beginning – there is so much that needs explaining ...*

Jamie had never actually met a parrot that could talk
before, but this parrot could not only talk but it had a
lisp and couldn't say its 'r's properly. 'I am your fwend,' it
said, and fixed Jamie with a beady eye. Jamie gazed back
into the black obsidian-like eye, almost hypnotized.

'I like you too,' he replied.

The parrot walked up the inside of its cage, the way
parrots do, and hung from the roof. It stared at Jamie
with its other eye, clicked its tongue, stretched its
wings and then said, 'My name is Nemethith.'

'Nemesis,' repeated Jamie.

The parrot began screeching furiously, clattering
its wings against the bars of the cage. 'Nemethith!'
squawked the enraged bird. 'Nemethith!'

'Keep your feathers on,' muttered Jamie crossly.

The parrot lunged forward, grabbing one of Jamie's fingers in its beak.

'Ow! Let go, you monster!'

'I am your fwend,' hissed Nemesis through his clenched beak.

'No you're not. Let go!' At last Jamie managed to wrench his hand away from the cage. He examined his finger. There were two purple welts, clear marks of the parrot's powerful beak. Jamie shook his hand in pain and rubbed the finger. At least there was no blood. He shot an angry glance at the bird. Parrots cannot smile, but Nemesis was doing a pretty good impression. Maybe it was the peculiar shape of the beak. Both the upper and lower mandibles had a single raised point on each side. Strange, thought Jamie.

*At first I thought it would be fun to have a pet parrot, especially one that could talk. Nemesis is a South American Paradise Parrot. He bit me on the very first day I got him. He bit Mum and Dad too. I suppose I should have started worrying at that point, but how was I to know that horror was just around the corner? If it hadn't been for that little mirror I might never have known, but I'd better fill in a bit more detail first ...*

The parrot had come from Jamie's aunt, who had seen him in a pet shop. Aunt Cleo was immediately seduced by the parrot's fabulous colouring, the black glitter of his eyes and the wonderful way in which he greeted Cleo's entrance into the shop. 'Hail to Her Majethty, Empweth of the Fowetht!'

Aunt Cleo bought the parrot on the spot, despite the fact that she was always going away on business and so couldn't be around to look after it much. She gave it to Jamie's family to care for instead. Aunt Cleo was like that. She was always buying animals and then giving them to Jamie's family. So far they had a giant lop-eared rabbit ( *Cleo: 'It's got ears like blankets!'* ), a chameleon ( *Cleo: You'll never have another fly in the house!* ), a llama they kept in the garden ( *Cleo: A llama is the best burglar deterrent you can have, in fact it's a burglar allarma!* ), and now a parrot.

But Nemesis was different. For a start he could speak, and then there were those dark eyes, as dark as the depths of a tropical rain forest by night; a darkness haunted by the soft footfall of the passing jaguar, and the silent slither of the anaconda. There was something of the night in Nemesis, especially the way he skulked in his cage, cracking open sunflower seeds and spitting the shells at Jamie while he slept. Then he'd whisper, 'I am your fwend.'

Jamie tried to teach Nemesis some *new* words. In revenge for the bite on his finger Jamie began with,

'Around the ragged rocks the ragged rascal ran.' This of course came out as, 'Awound the wagged wocks,' which was as far as Nemesis got, before clicking his tongue in disapproval and hanging upside down. Jamie had already learnt that this was usually a warning that the bird was about to have a temper tantrum. Sometimes the parrot seemed more human than bird.

Three days after the arrival of Nemesis, Jamie felt his injured finger itching and scratched it. That was when he first noticed the tiny fluff that had gathered round the edge of the bruising. He showed it to his mother.

'When your skin itches like that, it's a good sign. It shows that the cut is healing,' she said.

'My finger wasn't cut. It was just sort of – squeezed, very hard,' Jamie pointed out. 'By a parrot.'

His mother smiled brightly. 'I'm sure it's on the mend,' she insisted and clicked her tongue, as if to underline everything.

*It was not long after Nemesis bit me that other things began to happen.*

*The apple tree in the garden suddenly put on a growing spurt. It was early summer and I put it down to all the rain we'd been having but then the leaves began to enlarge. They fattened and lengthened and grew darker and denser. Day by day we watched the apple tree grow until it was*

*three times the size of our other trees. It dwarfed everything
around it. Mum and Dad thought it was wonderful, but
I thought it was weird, and then Dad actually climbed it
until he was sitting amongst the high branches. I was just
boggling at this when Mum suddenly whizzed up the tree
and joined him.*

*As for Nemesis, he spent all his time staring out
through the bars of his cage. He would make little
clucking noises and sometimes let out a long, growly sigh.
I thought that maybe he was bored ...*

One day Jamie was passing a pet shop and on a
sudden impulse he went in. He wondered what little
toys he might take home for the parrot to play with.
Nemesis must be getting pretty fed up, shut in a cage
most of the time. Jamie bought a bell and a mirror.
They were really meant for budgerigars but, as the pet
shop man said, parrots are just very big budgies really.

Nemesis hated the bell. He pulled it right off its
little chain and cast it out through the bars of the cage.
It rolled away under the sofa, where it stayed. So that
was the end of that.

As for the mirror, that was where the trouble began.
If it hadn't been for the mirror, Jamie might never have
known, never begun to wonder. Jamie was not sure
whether to bless or curse the mirror, but there was no

doubting its effect.

Nemesis did not seem at all bothered by the mirror. What Jamie noticed was this: when Nemesis looked in the mirror he didn't see a parrot looking back at him. He didn't see anything at all. *Nemesis didn't have a reflection.*

At first Jamie assumed that the mirror was no good and he went storming back to the pet shop. 'This mirror is defunct,' he said. 'It's not a mirror. It's a piece of glass.' But the pet shop man looked in it and saw himself and when Jamie took the trouble of peering in, he was there too.

Jamie, who by this time was not only puzzled but worried, returned home, took the parrot into the bathroom and held him up in front of the big mirror above the wash basin. Jamie was there, holding up his arm, but there was no parrot. Jamie paled. He knew there was only one creature that had no reflection in a mirror and that was a *vampire*.

As for Nemesis himself, he turned away from the mirror and gazed at Jamie with his eyes that were now like black holes in the fabric of space. 'I am your fwend,' he said, quietly.

Jamie was faced with the unpleasant observation that he was harbouring a vampire parrot – a vampire parrot with a speech impediment. Then he remembered his finger.

*It was when I noticed the tiny feathers on my finger*
*that I became seriously concerned. The fluff that had first*
*appeared around my bruise had now turned to feathers.*
*Of course they were very small; but they were also*
*unmistakeable. I couldn't show Mum and Dad because*
*I have hardly seen them since yesterday. I had to make*
*my own lunch and supper. They seem to spend all their*
*time up in the trees that have taken over our garden. The*
*trees sprang up overnight, a miniature rain forest. Some*
*of them are laden with exotic fruits that are eaten by the*
*troops of monkeys that race along the highest branches,*
*crashing amongst the dense leaves.*

*As for Nemesis, I swear he is now grinning at me. When*
*I went to sleep last night, I dreamt that he was talking to*
*me in a really sweet, kind voice, so smooth and soft. I would*
*wake, sweating, but he was always fast asleep in his cage ...*

Outside the house, monkeys whooped and howled.
Great birds sang and burbled amongst the dark branches,
and occasionally a glimpse of yellow and black signalled
the stealthy passing of the jaguar.

At night the parrot's eyes would snap open and
Nemesis would stare across at Jamie as he slept. Then
the parrot would begin his night whispers, in a soft,
crooning voice. 'Thoon you will be mine. Together

we thall wule the world. Thoon you will be a pawott like your pawenth. There ith no ethcape, for I am Nature'th methenger and it ith time for her to weclaim the world. Humanth have methed it up and now jungle thall cover the earth and all the wagged wocks wunth more and there will be no humanth at all. Ha ha ha ha.'

Jamie saw his parents one more time. They were sitting together on the branch of a tree at the edge of the spreading forest. Their clothes had gone and their bodies were covered in glowing feathers. Dad cocked his head on one side and gazed at Jamie, as if he were trying to remember who he was. They made their way down from the tree and stepped on to what was left of the lawn, but they wouldn't come any closer.

'Mum? Dad?' Jamie didn't know what to say.

His mother lifted one arm, as if she was inviting Jamie to join them. She clicked her tongue several times. Jamie's father opened his mouth and cawed. The hair on his head suddenly rose up in a crest and he cawed again. Then they went back into the forest. Jamie returned to the house on his own. He wandered into the kitchen and opened another packet of sunflower seeds. He began cracking them and spitting out the shells. They crunched beneath his feet: thousands of them, in every room.

*I try not to listen to Nemesis but it is becoming more and more difficult. Part of the problem is that I am now covered from head to foot with feathers. I can no longer wear clothes. Every now and then I get this uncontrollable urge to stand on the arm of the sofa, furiously flapping my arms, wanting to jump. I keep trying to walk up walls and hang from the light fittings.*

*I have tried all the usual vampire remedies but they don't seem to work on parrots. Nemesis seems to be invincible and every hour I become more like him.*

*What am I to do? The jungle has spread right the way down our street and across the park. I haven't seen another human for days.*

*Please help. You are my last hope. I cannot write any longer. It is too difficult to grip the pen with my thin claws. I am desperate. I looked in the mirror this morning and I wasn't there. Who am I? What am I? What is going to happen to me? I am your fwend. I am your fwend. I am ...*

# The Lobster's Birthday

## by Joan Aiken

Early one fine summer morning, two persons might have been seen making their way somewhat furtively across the fields from the village of Tillingham to Slugdale Halt. Every now and then they glanced cautiously behind them as if they almost expected to be pursued and taken back. Their names were Gloria and Harold. Gloria was a lobster. It was her birthday and she had persuaded Harold, who was a horse and an acquaintance of hers, to take her into Brighton for the day. The difficulty was that their employer did not approve of days off; he never took one himself and did not see why other people had to go gadding away, spending money, when they might just as well have stayed quietly at home and behaved themselves. Consequently, Gloria and Harold had to leave very early, as they had gone without permission and were still afraid that Mr Higgs might see them from some window as he stood drinking his early morning tea.

When they reached the station, which was in a cutting, Harold heaved a sigh of relief.

'Thank goodness we can have a bit of a breather,' he said. 'Mr Higgs can't see us here.' He sat down on the station seat, which sagged under his weight. Gloria seated herself primly beside him. She carried a large wicker basket and wore a festive spotted scarf.

'Dear me, I'm ever so warm. The weather is quite oppressive, isn't it,' she said. Then she looked reprovingly at her companion and exclaimed 'Harold! Put your shoes back on. What will people think of you! I declare I'm quite ashamed of you.'

'All very well to talk,' mumbled Harold. 'You made me wear these confounded shoes. Knew they'd be too tight in this weather.'

However, Gloria insisted that he must put them on again and he finally did so with many protests and hobbled off to buy two cheap day returns to Brighton.

At length the little train came in sight and Gloria immediately began to fuss, running up and down the platform, retying her veil, rearranging everything in her basket and clamouring that she had lost her gloves, while Harold stood expressionlessly in one spot and tried to look as if he had nothing to do with her. When the train stopped she cried, 'Oh, Harold, we must find a non-smoker. You know I can't stand cigarette smoke.' Without saying a word, Harold opened the nearest door and pushed her in. She subsided in a heap on the seat with her things all round her. Harold slumped down in the opposite seat and at once pulled a paper from under his arm and became absorbed in the racing news.

When Gloria had collected herself a little she began to chatter. 'Harold, do you think we could have the window down a little? This smoke gets in my eyes terribly. Do you think these people would mind?'

There were two other people in the compartment, a man and a woman, who both had their eyes shut. However, the man murmured, 'Not a bit, go ahead', without opening his eyes, so Harold opened the window a few inches.

'Now I think when we get there, I'll go right away and buy my new hat,' Gloria went on. 'What sort of a hat would you like me to have, Harold?'

'Don't mind a bit,' said Harold, his nose in the paper.

'I like a nice *fancy* hat,' said Gloria happily. 'Not too big, you know, but striking. What they call flair, a hat's got to have, if it's going to suit me. Mrs Ellis was telling me about a place right on the front, called *Natty Hats*, it is. I thought I might go there first.'

'All right,' said Harold, 'but I'm not going in one of those places. I should feel a fool. I'll go and have my hair cut while you get yourself suited.'

The woman asleep at the other end of the compartment, who had stirred a little at the mention of hats, now opened her eyes and let out a shriek.

'Percival!' she exclaimed. 'Pull the communication cord at once. There's a horse in the carriage!' Then she saw Gloria and screamed again.

'Pray calm yourself, Madam,' said the horse patiently. 'I am quite harmless, I assure you.'

But the woman kept exclaiming and would have pulled the cord herself if her husband had not stopped her.

'Don't make a fool of yourself, Minnie,' he said crossly. 'Bad enough to have to travel with horses and riff-raff without becoming a laughing-stock. Sit down, do, for heaven's sake.'

'I shall write to *The Times*,' his wife kept protesting. 'They ought at least to have No Horses carriages. As for lobsters, there ought to be a law against their travelling in trains. Pushing in where they're not wanted. What business have lobsters in trains?'

Gloria gave her a spiteful look. 'Some people seem to think they own the whole railway,' she said to Harold. 'They might like to know that other people, who have quite as much right to travel, only want to keep themselves to themselves and wouldn't demean themselves by intruding.'

Harold looked anxiously at the woman. 'Madam,' he began.

'Don't speak to me,' said the woman vigorously. '*Don't* speak to me or I shall scream, I know I shall.'

'But madam,' Harold began again.

'Percival, *will* you tell this person not to molest me. If you utter a single word more to me I shall have you given in charge the moment we get to Brighton.'

The horse shrugged his shoulders and settled back to his paper. Gloria drew herself up coldly and looked out of the window. The woman gave them a baleful glare, while her husband tried to dissociate himself from the whole affair.

Twenty minutes later, the train arrived in Brighton. During the whole of this time the woman had kept Harold and Gloria under constant observation, as if she expected one of them to throw a bomb the minute her back was turned.

When she stood up to collect her things together she let out a cry of horror. 'Percival! My knitting! The wool has fallen out of the window.'

'That is what I have been trying to tell you, madam,' said Harold calmly. 'It fell out at Bishopsvalley Halt, fifteen minutes ago.'

As Harold and Gloria left the platform they looked back and saw her standing at the very furthest extremity, furiously winding, while ten miles of wool came slowly towards her.

They took a bus down to the front and Gloria went at once into *Natty Hats*.

'And hurry up,' Harold called after her. 'I want a cuppa. I didn't have my tea this morning on account of you and your blessed treat.' Gloria ignored him and walked haughtily through the door. Madame Arlene at once glided forward to serve her.

'Mademoiselle requires a hat?'

'Something nice and fancy,' said Gloria, her eye roaming greedily round the display stands.

'But Mademoiselle is rather short and has – ahem – rather a *bright* complexion. Would not something more simple – we have here a black velvet beret with diamond clip, price fifteen guineas?'

'Now, now,' said Gloria, 'none of your taste for me, thanks. I want something nice and bright, with feathers.' Madame Arlene brought out several other hats, but none of them seemed quite what she wanted, and she was presently aware of Harold, looking very cross, strolling up and down outside. He had had his hair cut and looked very military.

'Oh well, I'll leave it, thanks ever so,' said Gloria and scuttled out. 'No need to make me conspicuous,' she scolded Harold. 'You could have waited a bit further along, couldn't you?'

When they had had a cup of tea, however, sitting in deckchairs, good humour was restored and Harold suggested that they should go on the pier before Gloria looked at any more hats. So they paid their money and clicked through the turnstile.

Gloria had her fortune told by the Seer from the East – Put One Penny in and Learn the Secrets of the Stars. She put in a penny and pulled out a piece of paper which said, 'You will be your own fate today'. 'Stupid things they tell you, don't they,' she said, tossing it into the sea. Then she suddenly squealed, 'Oo! Look, Harold! Over there!'

She was pointing to the display stand of a shooting gallery. Among the prizes offered were some feather dusters, with red handles and gay red and purple feathers.

'Just what I want for my hat! They might have been made for me. Oh, do have a go and win one of them, Harold,' she urged him. Harold rather unwillingly went over to the booth.

'Eight shots for half a crown,' said the man, looking at him suspiciously. 'Never heard of a horse shooting before.'

'I don't suppose you often see horses on the pier at all,' Harold replied coldly. 'I'll have eight shots please. How many bullseyes to win a prize?'

'Three,' the man told him. Gloria was teetering about behind him in such a state of excitement that he made her go away – he said the sound of her claws on the iron treads made him nervous. So she went and stood round the corner clutching her basket feverishly. As a matter of fact, Harold had never shot before, but he often took part in a game of darts and he was very anxious not to let Gloria down, so he aimed with great care.

'Eight bulls,' said the proprietor. 'Blimey! On the halls, are yer? What'll you have for your prizes?'

'I'd like two of those dusters, please.'

'Better make it three for luck,' said the man cordially. 'Any time you want to give a display, just let me know and I'll fix it up for you.'

Harold took Gloria the trophies and she squeaked with pleasure. 'Three! Harold, you are a dear!' She was about to embrace him, but he backed cautiously away. She stuck the feathers on her head and rushed off to find a mirror and admire herself.

After this they began to feel hungry and found a sheltered seat where they could eat their sandwiches – grass for Harold and mayonnaise for Gloria. Then

Harold wanted to sleep, but Gloria began to fidget and suggested they should go for a trip in the *Skylark* to see the Seven Sisters.

'All right,' Harold agreed. 'I can sleep in the boat as well as anywhere else, I suppose.'

Off they went. Gloria had never been in a boat before and sat bolt upright, giving little cries of pleasure and excitement at everything and taking care that everyone could see and admire her beautiful plumes. Alas! As they went further out to sea the wind freshened and a sudden gust whisked all three off her head and overboard.

'Stop the boat!' shrieked Gloria. 'My hat!'

'Sorry, miss,' said the owner. 'Should have fastened it on better. No hope of getting it now.'

'Harold!' she cried in despair. 'My hat!' But Harold was nearly asleep and only grumbled, 'Expect me to dive after it? Did you ever hear of a horse swimming?'

Poor Gloria took a last frantic look round and then dived in herself. She managed to seize two of the feathers and then the propeller of the *Skylark* struck her on the head and she knew no more. Harold had fallen into a blissful doze and never noticed that she was no longer beside him.

Presently, a girl who was swimming near the shore espied a lobster floating near her.

'Coo! Here's a bit of luck,' she said. 'This'll do nicely for supper.' She towed the unconscious Gloria in to land and popped her into a beach bag with some sun-tan lotion, dark glasses and peppermint creams. 'I'll just get my things on and pop into Arlene's and then I'll be stepping home. Mum will be pleased.'

As soon as she was dressed, she went into *Natty Hats*, where one of the assistants was a friend of hers. Business was slack just then and she began gossiping with this girl. Meanwhile the powerful fragrance of the peppermint creams partly revived Gloria and she crawled out of the bag in search of fresh air and lay weakly down on a large straw cartwheel hat. By and by a woman came into the shop and began trying on hats.

'How much is the straw?' she enquired.

'Five guineas, madam,' said the assistant, without turning round.

'Very well, I'll take it. You needn't bother to wrap it, I'll wear it. Rather attractive and original, don't you think, Percival?' she said, turning to her husband. He merely shuddered, but she took no notice and put down five guineas on the cash desk. Then she and her husband left the shop and began strolling along the front.

Meanwhile the *Skylark* had put back to shore and its owner woke up Harold, who stumbled up the beach in a dazed condition, without noticing that his companion was not there. He walked along the front and soon noticed a commotion ahead of him. The warm sunshine was reviving Gloria and she began waving her claws about and putting herself to rights before she became aware that she was on a moving platform. People gazed admiringly at this remarkable hat ornamented with a live lobster and soon a small crowd was following, while the woman who had bought it still walked underneath quite unconscious of what was happening.

Harold saw them coming towards him and his eyes bulged. 'Gloria!' he said. 'What are you doing up there?'

'Oh!' shrieked the woman. 'It's that horse again. Take it away. Everywhere I go today it's nothing but horses, horses.'

'But, madam,' said Harold, always polite, 'you have my partner on your hat. If you will excuse me one moment, I will assist her to alight.'

'Harold, where am I?' said Gloria faintly.

'Do you mean there is a real lobster on this hat?' cried the woman underneath. 'This is a gross swindle. I paid five guineas for it. I shall take it back to the shop and complain.'

At this moment the representative of the *Brighton Guardian* arrived.

'Please stand still for a moment while I take some pictures,' he begged them. 'This will be quite a sensation. Dashing Dowager Displays Live Lobster on Hat. May I congratulate you, madam? You are the fortunate winner of our Original Headgear Competition. Your prize is a Rolls Royce and a free pass to the Magnificent Cinema every night for the next five years. May I ask where you obtained this novel creation?'

Much mollified by this news, the woman told him that she had bought it at *Natty Hats*.

'This will mean a boom for Arlene,' said the reporter. 'Why, here she comes now.' In fact Arlene, her assistant and the assistant's friend were hastening along the front, having just discovered that the lobster had been stolen.

'Good afternoon,' the reporter greeted them. 'You will be pleased to learn that your creation here has just won the Original Headgear Prize. Can you tell me if you have any other ideas in the same line – a salad hat, perhaps, or a calves' foot toque[1]?'

While the explanations were going on, Gloria beckoned to Harold.

'Do you think you could lift me down,' she whispered weakly. 'I feel a little faint.'

He did so quietly, without anyone noticing. 'Let's get out of here while they're all talking,' he muttered. 'It's

---

[1] A type of hat.

nearly time for our train and Mr Higgs won't like it at all if we get our names in the papers.' Gloria nodded and he cantered off up a side street, carrying her on his back. By the time their absence was noticed, they were well away. Madame Arlene offered to replace the bare straw hat by another and everyone parted happily, except the girl who had hoped to have lobster for supper.

Gloria and Harold stopped to have a refreshing cup of tea on their way to the station and after all only just caught their train. They flung themselves into the last carriage, and only realized after the train had started that they were again in the same compartment with Percival and his wife. She was now wearing a very gorgeous hat, covered with red bouncing cherries.

She gave Gloria and Harold a haughty look and then decided to ignore them. Harold was feeling tired and longing to be back at home and to go quietly to bed. Gloria was still a little faint after her experiences and insisted on leaning out of the window, in spite of the notice warning her not to.

'You know I can't stand the cigarette smoke,' she said reproachfully.

When they were nearing Slugdale Halt she took out her pocket mirror to adjust her red feathers.

'Oh! They've gone!' she cried in dismay. 'Where are my beautiful feathers?'

'They fell off at Bishopsvalley Halt fifteen minutes ago,' said Percival's wife acidly. Gloria shed a few tears and then cheered up.

'Oh well, I suppose I was fated not to have them,' she said philosophically. 'It looks that way. And anyway, who ever heard of a lobster wearing a hat?'

She gave Percival and his wife a dazzling smile and let Harold help her out of the train. They strolled off across the fields towards Tillingham Village and the Horse and Lobster Inn.

# About the authors

**Morris Gleitzman** is one of Australia's most successful authors. He started by writing films and TV scripts, but then discovered you can get closer to a character's thoughts and feelings in a book than in a film.

**Russell Hoban** (1925–2011) was a much-admired writer for both adults and children. His best-known books are *Riddley Walker*, *The Mouse and His Child* and the *Frances* series.

**Richmal Crompton** (1890–1969) was most famous as the author of the *Just William* series. William first appeared in a book in 1922, but he still lives on – both in books and in films and TV series!

**Philip K. Dick** (1928–1982) was a brilliant American science fiction writer. His most famous book (for adults) was *Do Androids Dream of Electric Sheep?*, which was later made into the film *Blade Runner*.

**Alan Garner** is a highly respected author for children and adults. He is probably best known for his children's fantasy novels, including *The Weirdstone of Brisingamen*, and his retellings of British folk tales.

**Geoffrey Willans and Ronald Searle** were co-creators of the anarchic *Molesworth* series, about the irrepressible Nigel Molesworth and his career at the school from hell, St Custard's.

**Jeremy Strong** says he has the best job ever! He spends most of his time writing and visiting schools, libraries and festivals. He is the author of many hilarious best-selling books, including *The Hundred-Mile-An-Hour Dog* and *Krazy Kow Saves the World*.

**Joan Aiken** (1924–2004) wrote more than 100 books full of magic, mythology, fantasy and adventure. Among her best-known series for children are the *Wolves of Willoughby Chase* books.